DROPSHIPPING MADE EASY

Build And Scale Your Dropshipping Business

Ed Sherman

Table of Contents

Introduction 1

Chapter 1: The Basics of Dropshipping 3

Chapter 2: The Tools That You Need 11

Chapter 3: How Do I Get My Products? 15

Chapter 4: Choosing Your Products 25

Chapter 5: Which Sales Channels are the Best for My Business 33

Chapter 6: Running Your Business 41

Conclusion 49

© Copyright 2017 by Phoenix Publishing - All rights reserved.

The following book is reproduced below with the goal of providing information that is as accurate and reliable as possible. Regardless, purchasing this book can be seen as consent to the fact that both the publisher and the author of this book are in no way experts on the topics discussed within and that any recommendations or suggestions that are made herein are for entertainment purposes only. Professionals should be consulted as needed prior to undertaking any of the action endorsed herein.

This declaration is deemed fair and valid by both the American Bar Association and the Committee of Publishers Association and is legally binding throughout the United States.

Furthermore, the transmission, duplication or reproduction of any of the following work including specific information will be considered an illegal act irrespective of if it is done electronically or in print. This extends to creating a secondary or tertiary copy of the work or a recorded copy and is only allowed with express written consent from the Publisher. All additional right reserved.

The information in the following pages is broadly considered to be a truthful and accurate account of facts and as such any inattention, use or misuse of the information in question by the reader will render any resulting actions solely under their purview. There are no scenarios in which the publisher or the original author of this work can be in any fashion deemed liable for any hardship or damages that may befall them after undertaking information described herein.

Additionally, the information in the following pages is intended only for informational purposes and should thus be thought of as universal. As befitting its nature, it is presented without assurance regarding its prolonged validity or interim quality. Trademarks that are mentioned are done without written consent and can in no way be considered an endorsement from the trademark holder.

Introduction

Congratulations on downloading this book and thank you for doing so.

The following chapters will discuss some of the basics of dropshipping and how you can get started with this great business endeavor. This is a great business to get into because of the low cost and low risk, but there is a lot of competition so you need to be ready to take it on and handle all of the other sellers who will be there too. This guidebook will help you to go from beginner to expert in dropshipping so you can see the best results.

In this guidebook, we are going to take the time to talk about the different parts of your dropshipping business. We started out with some of the basics and the benefits that come with dropshipping and then moved on to how to pick out the company you want to work with, how to pick out the right product, and even how to determine which sales channel is going to be the right one for you.

There are many different aspects that come with dropshipping, but this can make it a lot of fun for the entrepreneur who wants to get in on the fun and the profit. When you are ready to get started with dropshipping, make sure to check out this guidebook to help you out!

DROPSHIPPING MADE EASY

There are plenty of books on this subject on the market, thanks again for choosing this one! Every effort was made to ensure it is full of as much useful information as possible, please enjoy!

Chapter 1:

The Basics of Dropshipping

Before you jump into this line of business, it is important to understand what dropshipping is all about. Dropshipping is the practice of fulfilling orders in a way that the retailer is not going to store or ship the products themselves. The supplier or the distributor will store and ship all the goods for the retailer, but the retailer will do all of the marketing and bring the customers in. This can be a very effective way to make money for a lot of dropshippers because it will reduce their costs and the risks that they take, while also being pretty convenient and practical for them to use.

So, how does this process really work? If you are a dropshipper, you are going to list the product that you want to sell online. A customer will find that product and then place an order for it online. Once you receive that order, as well as the payment that comes with it, your job will be to take that information, contact the wholesaler, and purchase the product for the customer. The product will then be sent directly to the customer.

To make money on this, you will need to charge a little bit more on the product than the wholesaler is selling it for. You can then keep the extra for your time and effort. It is usually going to be a small amount of profit on each product, but if you sell a lot of products, you can make some good money.

The nice thing is that you will not be the one in charge of holding onto the product or shipping it out. You will just take the information that the customer sends to you and then place the order for them. the wholesaler is going to send the product over to the customer for you. This takes out some of your risks, but make sure that you pick out a good wholesaler who will send out orders promptly and will provide good customer service.

How do I get started?

Working in dropshipping is relatively easy to get started with, which is why there is a lot of competition. Luckily for you, there are a lot of people who think that this is something they never have to spend time on and they will quit pretty early on in the game. This leaves a lot of openings for you to see success if you follow the right tips and keep moving forward with your business.

To start, you need to decide what supplier you would like to use. The supplier is going to be the company that makes and stores the products you would like to sell. They will also do all of the shipping for you so picking out a good one is so important to ensure that you can provide great customer service each time. It is possible to pick out a few different suppliers if you find some that are good for the various products that you would like to sell, but it is important to make sure that you are going with a company that is reputable and will be able to help you do your job well.

Chapter 1: The Basics of Dropshipping

Once you have picked out a supplier, it is time to pick out the products that you want to work with. It is a good idea to work with a few different products at a time to help increase your profit margins, but do not go too crazy when you are first getting started because that can be a lot to take on. Rather, pick a handful of products, probably ones that go together well and could maybe use upselling to make a bigger profit, to keep things as simple as possible.

Now it is time to pick out how much you are going to sell those items for. You will need to take a look at the price of the items from your supplier and determine if you will be able to make a profit off these. Take a look at the prices that the item is going for online and see how big of a profit margin you will be able to make. You may be surprised that some items have a large profit margin and others are pretty low and not worth your time.

At this point, it is time to list the items. There are a few different options that you can go with here. Some people like to go with Amazon and eBay because all of the SEO is taken care of for them. There isn't much personalization that comes with these options though, and they can be hard to beat out the competition. Using your own personal website and social media can take a bit more work to get started with, but they give tremendous results.

From here you are just going to wait for a customer to place an order. Once they do, you will take the information that they provide and use it to place the order with your supplier. If you did it right, the customer would give you all the information that you need for this transaction, and you will get a bit of money on top of the cost, which is your profit.

The supplier will receive this information from you and will send the product straight over to the customer. You are never going to see the product, which is part of the fun because it will save you some of the inventory and the risk and can speed up the shipping process since a second stop does not need to be added in.

With each product, you are probably not going to make a ton of money. But if you can do your marketing well and make a lot of sales, you are going to end up with a good profit overall. The amount of profit that you can make depends on the products that you choose to go with, how much profit margin there is, and how good you are at selling these products and getting the customers in. Dropshippers love this business because there are no limits to how much they can make.

In addition, the supplier is going to love this method because they are selling products in the process. They do not need to worry about marketing and spending that money, which is something that a lot of the dropshipping suppliers are not that great with. Instead, they get to concentrate on inventory and sending out the product, while you take care of the rest for them. It is a win-win for both parties involved.

The Benefits of Dropshipping

There are a lot of great benefits that come from starting your own dropshipping business. It is a great way for you to sell products without having to worry about inventory or all of the risk, and then the manufacturer, or your supplier, will be able to sell more products without having to pay upfront for that advertising that you do.

Chapter 1: The Basics of Dropshipping

This is beneficial for both you and for the wholesaler. The wholesaler will not have to spend money advertising their products and trying to bring in customers. The dropshipper is going to do some of that work for them, saving them a lot of time and money. There are also a lot of benefits that you will notice from joining this business as well including:

- Offer many different products: when you work in this industry, you can sell a ton of different products compared to what you could do if you had to keep an inventory of everything. Think of how many things you would have to store in your home to be successful in this business. You would really need to limit yourself if you did this. But since you are not responsible for stocking or holding onto inventory, you can choose what types and how many products you would like to sell.

- Lower risk: compared to some other business ideas, working in dropshipping can have less risk. This is because you will not need to hold onto inventory and there aren't any upfront costs that you need to deal with. For the most part, the only thing that you will lose out on if this is not successful for you is the cost of starting your own website, which is pretty low for starting a business.

- Low cost: you never have to make an investment to get started with dropshipping. You can choose to set up a personal website if you would like, but you can also use Amazon and other sites and keep your startup costs down to nothing.

- More time: if you stick with dropshipping, you can make the same money that you would with running your own business, but you do not need to stack, store, receive, pack, pull, or ship the items at all. Since these are really time-consuming activities, you will save yourself some of the hassle and time when you start this business.

- Can work from anywhere: your location does not matter when it comes to this business. All that you need is some good customer service skills to talk to your customers and suppliers, a good internet connection, and to make sure that you pick out some good suppliers.

- Scalable: the nice thing about this business is that the majority of the work is going to fall to the suppliers. You will put in the sales work, but you do not have to worry about shipping or holding onto inventory for the product.

- Easy to start: you will find that it does not take that much time or effort to get started in the dropshipping and almost anyone can do so. You just need to pick out some good products that are easy to sell and list them for a good price, and you are ready to go.

- Pick the markets that you want: there are instances when trying to get a product across international borders is going to be too hard to do. However, if you work with the right supplier, it is possible to do this in a cost-effective way. The result is an opportunity for you

Chapter 1: The Basics of Dropshipping

to be able to test out a new market and determine if it is the right one for you.

As you can see, there are quite a few good benefits that come from starting your own drop shipping business. You only have to be the salesperson, but if you are successful, you can reach people all over the country, and even all over the world, and make some profits from that. And since the suppliers are going to do all the packaging and shipping for you, you will not have to spend a ton of time on this endeavor to see results.

Chapter 2:

The Tools That You Need

Now that you know some of the benefits of starting a dropshipping company and you are ready to begin, it is time to make sure that you have all the tools that are needed to really see some success. This is a relatively easy business, but you do need to make sure that all the pieces are in place before you get started. Luckily, with the help of the information in this chapter, you will be able to gather all the right tools and get everything in place in no time.

The first thing that you need is a supplier. This is the business where you will purchase all of the items that you want to list and make a profit from. The good news is that there are quite a few reliable suppliers for you to choose from. The biggest determinant is finding the one that offers the products you want to sell at the best price. It is a good idea to find a supplier who has a good reputation, has been doing dropshipping for a long time and is sure to be a good business partner in the future.

The next thing that you need to focus on is the right products. It is much better to only sell two or three really good products rather than selling ten bad products and wasting all of that time. You need to go with good products, ones that have a good audience already and can be easier to sell.

There are a lot of ways that you can choose which products you want to sell. Some people choose to sell items that are considered best sellers. This can give you a wide audience, but remember that there are a lot of other people who are trying to sell these products as well, so the competition is fierce. You can also choose to go with a product that you like, or that has captured your interest, just make sure that you do a bit of market research first to see if this product has a chance of becoming successful.

You also need to make sure that you have a Tax ID. This is like a retail license, and it is going to be required by most suppliers before you do any transactions with them. This is also important if you are trying to do transactions in the United States or Canada. Some states will allow you to just use your social security number to conduct business, so check up on your laws to see what you need. If you live in a state that needs this ID, it is pretty easy and inexpensive to get one.

Next on the list is a selling platform. You need to not only pick out the product that you want to work with, but you need to also figure out where you would like to sell that product from. There are a lot of o options that you can choose from, but make sure that you do not end up spreading yourself too thin in the process.

One site that a lot of dropshippers like to use is eBay. There are many other auctions like sites that work well too, and many will go on reputable sites like Amazon as well. Another option is for you to make your own website. This can be a good

Chapter 2: The Tools That You Need

idea if you would like to sell several similar products and with the help of SEO, you can really get the attention of some of your potential customers.

You also need to get an EIN number to work as a dropshipper. This is a requirement that the IRS has set out for all businesses because it is like the social security number for your business. It is going to help you out a lot when it comes to opening up a business bank account, applying for your account as a dropshipper, and even when filing taxes.

Another thing that you may want to consider is to use some financial platforms. It is never a good idea to combine your business finances with your personal finances. This means that it is a good idea to set up your own financial accounts that you will only use with your business. Consider setting up a business checking account to make things easier.

Note that it is best if you can run all of the finances for your business into one checking account. Then you can deposit all the revenues that you get from the business, and you have a safe and secure place to pay for any business expenses that come up. It just makes it easier to keep track of the transactions that happen for your business and the ones that happen in your personal life when you keep the two things separate. You can also consider getting a business credit card or debit card if you would like.

Social media can also be a great thing for you to look into when getting started. Remember that as a dropshipper, you are basically going to be the marketing for these products and then you can make a profit off the products that you sell. Social media is a great way to get the word out about your products and to reach a broader audience than you can all on your own.

The good news is that there are a ton of social media accounts that you can choose to go with. many people like to use Facebook and a few of the other big ones, but you do need to consider the products that you are trying to sell. Some are going to do well with more descriptions while others will sell better with some good pictures.

Make sure that you do not spread yourself too thin when it comes to working on social media. There is a plethora of social media sites that you can choose from, but if you pick too many, you will spend too much time working on the social media and not enough time actually helping your customers or running your business at all. It is best to stick with two maybe three social media sites and spend your time and energy working with customers on there.

As you can see, there are a few things that you need to have in place to start your dropshipping business. They are pretty simple things, and the good news is, they are not going to cost you a lot of money to get them done. This is one of the best benefits of working in the dropshipping industry; you can get started with making some good money without having to spend a lot of money upfront to get started.

Chapter 3:

How Do I Get My Products?

The next thing that we need to focus on is how to get your products. To start with dropshipping, you need to be able to pick out the products that you would like to list and sell, and you are going to get these products from a good wholesaler or a supplier. Finding the right one is going to make a big difference in how successful you are as a dropshipper. This is because they are going to be in charge of customer service, sending out the product, and how good the product is to start with. There are a few things that you can look out for when it comes to finding the best supplier for your business and we are going to take a look at them in this guidebook.

Know your industry

The first thing that you need to do is be aware of the industry that you want to join. There are many industries that are going to come with their own supply chains, and you need to understand these industries to know where you fit into the puzzle. This makes it easier for you to find the suppliers that you need because you can look for the ones that will cater to what you want to do.

For example, let's say that you want to start your own boutique that is going to sell specialized items. You are probably not going to do the best with this if you decide to get in contact with some of the larger distributors. On the other hand, you will see some more success if you choose to go with a supplier that is smaller and perhaps more local.

Try out your manufacturer ahead of time

A good place to get started is to contact a manufacturer that you would like to use and ask if they are willing to work with dropshipping. It is best to do this over the phone because it can help you to get direct contact and get all your questions answered right away. This is a good thing to do if you are trying to get into a new or small niche.

Whenever you contact a new manufacturer, you need to check and see if they actually do dropshipping. Not all manufacturers, no matter how big or small they are, are going to offer their items like this. But calling them ahead of time can make it easier to figure out the ones that are right for you.

Look on Google

If you are still looking for some good wholesalers to work with, go ahead and do a search on Google or online. This method can pose some difficulties though. There is a lot that will post online and will advertise their products, but most of them are not going to be that great. In fact, the best wholesalers to work with, the ones that won't ask for a lot of money upfront and won't try to mess things up, are not that great at marketing, so it is hard to find them with a simple search.

Chapter 3: How Do I Get My Products?

This does not mean that the cause is hopeless online. You just need to realize that the good companies are not going to be within the first few listings on a search engine. Keep going through and using the right targeted terms, and you will be able to find the company that you would like to use.

Order from the competition

Ordering products from a few different dropshippers can help you to figure out who will be the best supplier for you to pick from. In the beginning, you will maybe look at a few different wholesalers and not be able to tell who is the best. But when you actually place an order with them, you get the chance to see how they treat their customers, how fast the order comes in, and other important information that will make it easier to make your decision.

Ordering from a few wholesalers can help as well. You will be able to compare these factors, as well as price, and see who has the best options. You get to be the customer in a way that is hard to do in other ways, and you can determine if the company is going to provide you with the customer service and a good product for you to enjoy.

Look at supplier directories

If you would like to get started in dropshipping, you may be curious to know if it is worth your time to look and spend money on a supplier directory. The supplier directory is going to be a database that has all the suppliers you can choose from based on their market, niche, product and other factors.

This may seem like an expense that you do not need, but it is going to make sure that you are using suppliers who are legitimate and will be good to work with. All of the suppliers who are on these lists have been screened, so you know they provide you with legitimate opportunities. You can pay a small fee to look at the list (which is a fee for the site that built up the directory, not to the suppliers themselves) and then get a full list at your fingertips to use.

Another benefit of using this directory is that it will make it easier to brainstorm some ideas for the market or niche that you want to enter into and start selling with. It is beneficial to making some of the decisions that you need along the way.

There are a number of different supplier directories, and a comprehensive review of all of them is beyond the scope of this guide. Instead, I'll highlight some of the most well-known directories online.

Worldwide Brands

Established 1999

Thousands of wholesalers

Over 10 million products

Price: $299 for a lifetime membership

Worldwide Brands is one of the oldest and best-known supplier directories. It advertises that it only includes suppliers that meet a set of guidelines to ensure legitimate, quality wholesalers.

This directory does include a large collection of legitimate wholesalers. If you want lifetime access to a quality directory and are comfortable with a larger one-time payment, Worldwide Brands is a safe bet.

Chapter 3: How Do I Get My Products?

SaleHoo

Established 2005

Over 8,000 suppliers

Price: $67 per year

The SaleHoo supplier directory lists more than 8,000 bulk purchase and dropshipping suppliers, and seems to cater heavily to merchants on eBay, and Amazon.

SaleHoo's $67 annual price is one of the most compelling values among supplier directories and includes a 60-day money-back guarantee. If you're comfortable paying an annual membership – or only need to use a directory temporarily, SaleHoo might be worth a look.

Doba

Established 2002

165 suppliers

Over 1.5 million products

Price: $60 per month

Instead of simply listing suppliers, Doba's service integrates with dropshippers (hence why they only have 165 suppliers) allowing you to place orders with multiple warehouses using its centralized interface. Membership also includes a Push-to-Marketplace tool that automates the process of listing items on eBay.

Doba's centralized system offers more convenience then the other directories. If you place a high value on convenience and can find the products you want among their suppliers, Doba's interface may be worth the cost.

However, if you can identify quality suppliers on your own and don't mind working with them directly, you'll be able to save around $700 / year. If there are only a few key suppliers in your niche – reducing the number of parties you have to coordinate with – this may be the way to go.

Wholesale Central

Established 1996

1,400 suppliers

740,000 products

Price: free

Unlike many other directories, there's no charge to search Wholesale Central for suppliers because it charges suppliers a fee to be listed and also displays ads on their site. They also claim to review and screen all suppliers to ensure they are legitimate and trustworthy.

It's difficult to argue with free, and there's no harm in browsing the listings at Wholesale Central, but you'll need to be a bit more discriminating. A number of the suppliers appear to be retailers selling to the public at "wholesale" prices – not something a supplier would do when offering real wholesale pricing. So while there are genuine wholesale opportunities listed, you may want to be a little more thorough with your due diligence.

Chapter 3: How Do I Get My Products?

Ask for referrals

Once you start to find some suppliers, even if they end up not being the right ones for your niche or your needs, make sure to ask for referrals. They may not be right for you, but they can point you in the right direction of a supplier who may work. This is also a great way to gather some information and contacts in the beginning.

Avoiding scams

When you are going through your search to find a good supplier, it is important to learn how to identify good suppliers from the ones who are fraudulent. There are a lot of great companies out there who work with dropshipping because it helps them to save money on marketing while still selling their products. But there are also a lot of companies out there who just want to take your money and never help you earn at all. Since dropshipping can be extremely profitable, it is important to avoid these scams as much as possible.

The good news is that there are ways to spot a scam pretty easily. First, you need to look and see if you can find out any information about the wholesaler that you want to use. Are you able to find their full business name or the contact details? Legitimate companies are not going to try and hide this information, and they will make it easy to find.

You can also do some background information on the company. There are often reviews about a company, and you need to take a look at these. One thing to look at is whether the wholesaler is using replica goods or not. You want to make sure that you are getting legitimate goods, ones that will impress your customers. If you are unsure about the products that the wholesaler sends out, it is best to use someone else.

Another place to look is the payment methods. Many scammers are going to use things like Bitcoin or Western Union because they are hard to trace. You will put in the money and never hear back. And with no way to trace the money, it becomes impossible to ever get it back.

You can also spend some time calling the company. You want to make sure that you are working with a legitimate business, and giving the company a call is a good way to do this. Many companies that are scams will put up a fake number, and you will never be able to reach them. Not only do you need to make calls, but you also need to ask questions to make sure this company is legitimate. For example, if you would like to sell products in the computer niche, ask about the different computers or the processors or something like that. A good company will be able to answer your questions without any trouble.

And finally, when you are talking to the company you should see if they are willing to send out a sample order. Some wholesalers are going to ask you to have a minimum order instead, but some will let you try it out as a trial to make sure things work out well. This is a great way to verify that the company is a good one and that your customers will be treated properly if you use this company.

Picking out a good supplier can make or break your whole business. This is going to be the company that is going to send out the products and will do a lot of the interactions with your customers for you. Take your time to do the right research and

Chapter 3: How Do I Get My Products?

talk to the company, and you are sure to see the results that you want with dropshipping.

Chapter 4:

Choosing Your Products

Another thing that you need to consider when it comes to dropshipping is what kind of product that you would like to sell. There are so many different products that are available for this business, but you are not going to have the time or the energy to do all of the products so you need to pick what niche you would like to work on.

The good news is that with so many products that are available, you are sure to find the right niche that is popular and which you can make a lot of money with. The best thing that you can do is pick out one niche and then choose products that fall into it.

One mistake that you need to avoid during this time is to make choices based on your interests and your passions. Yes, you may know a lot about the product when you choose to go with this method, but it is not always the best way to sell a lot of products. You instead need to look into some market research and find products that not only sell well but which can make a good profit on top so you can earn money.

The good news is that there are a lot of different niches and products that you can work with. Some of the options that you may want to choose from to make a good profit out of your dropshipping business include:

Beauty products

These products are sure to make you a lot of money. And since people all over the world use beauty products, you can find a lot of potential customers. Selling beauty products can be a great experience, as long as you provide your customers with an experience that is unforgettable with fantastic and high-quality products and fast shipping straight away to the customer.

Dropshipping is perfect when it comes to selling beauty products. You can pick from a wide variety of products that you would like to work with, you can choose a reputable company, and you can provide an unforgettable experience to your customers.

Computer accessories

These are a great idea to sell because they allow you to add quite a bit of money on top of the original price and still sell them competitively. You may not sell as many units on these, but each one can make you a good amount of profit. There are a lot of people who are looking to update their technology all the time, and you can sell many additional components. For example, if you sell a computer, you can also sell the keyboard, headphones, a mouse, and so on.

Once your customer has placed an order, you will be able to use the process of dropshipping to send all of these products at once. You may have to work through a few different wholesalers to help out with this, but it can provide a great

Chapter 4: Choosing Your Products

experience to the customer. They may order a lot of different accessories with their product, but you can send it all at once and provide a superior customer service experience in the process.

Clothing

Another option that a lot of dropshippers like to work with is clothing. This is actually one of the most in-demand products on the market right now, and you can find a lot of customers as long as you are willing to diversify a little bit and provide some unique products. There is also a lot of potentials that come with this. Some customers may only purchase a single item from you that they need, but if you have a lot of variety, you will be able to get some people who will order their whole wardrobe from you.

If you are selling clothing of any kind to your customers, you need to work on making them have a great experience in the process. The whole process from looking at your website to ordering the item and even the shipping should be easy and fast to your customer so that they come back. Ensure that you add in some unique items, some that can be personalized even, and you will find a lot of interested customers with clothing.

Accessories

Accessories are also a good thing to work with when it comes to working with dropshipping. You will not make a lot of each one because the price is lower to start with, but it is a lot easier to sell a lot of these so you will make some good money in the process. and since you can use dropshipping to handle the packaging and shipping, you can send a lot of these products without wasting all of your own time and effort.

Books

Books are one of the most popular products to sell online, but having your own inventory of books is hard to handle. They can take up a lot of room and if you do not sell them, what are you going to do with all of the extra books. But with dropshipping, this is not going to be that big of an issue. You can sell whatever types of books that you would like, even a lot of different books, and you will do great.

Of course, these are just a few of the profitable products that you can choose when it comes to dropshipping. The important part is to do some market research and figure out what products are selling well and what you can make money from. There are a lot of products that do well, but there is a lot that does not do that well too and figuring out the difference between them can help you out.

Popularity of products

When you are deciding to sell certain products, you need to ask yourself whether you think that the product is actually going to sell or not. This is where the market research is going to come into play. There are a few good methods that you can use to figure this out. Looking at the trends online and elsewhere, such as visiting Amazon Bestsellers, is a great place to start.

You do not necessarily want to go with a product that is the most popular all of the time. This product is probably going to have a ton of people already selling it, and the competition can

Chapter 4: Choosing Your Products

make it really difficult to work with. On the other hand, if there is a product that you would like to sell and it has hardly any sales at all, it is probably not a good place to go.

You can also find a lot of niche products this way. There are always people who are looking to have a specialty product, or they are searching for something in a specific niche. You may not make a ton of sales like you might see on the bestsellers list, but there is going to be less competition, so you get the benefit of being able to get more of the customers in the process.

So, to keep things easy, we are going to use the Amazon Bestsellers list to help us determine what products to work with, but there are many other options that you can go with as well. Create a list of several products that you are interested in selling, and then go to this page to check the rankings. This will give you a good idea of how well the product would do on the market and whether this is the right one for you to use.

Check the prices

The next thing that you need to do is check the prices. Once you know what products you want to pursue, you need to figure out how much they are going for on the market. You can also look to see how many duplicate items are available for those same products. This allows you to compare the prices of various items. Some comparison shopping engines, like eBay and Etsy, will allow you to see the prices but check on the retail and the supplier prices.

As you are going through this, it is a good idea to set up a spreadsheet where you can place all this pricing information, ensuring that you do not have to remember it all. The sheet should have the name of the item you want to sell, the highest and lowest price of it, and the sales volume. You may need to go through and update this on occasion if things change, but it is a good way to see if the product is profitable and if you should go after it.

Study your profit margin

Using the step that we just went through, it is time to figure out how much profit you will be able to make from each product you want to use. Once you know how much the product is priced from the supplier and how much you can see it for online, you can get a good idea of how much profit there is to make with each product that you choose.

When you are examining the profit margin, a good place to start is at one hundred percent. This means that if you are not able to sell the item for two times the amount that you purchased the item for, you will be spending a lot of time doing the work without making a lot of money. Going for some of the higher priced items may be the best option for you because it helps you to earn a good chunk of money on each sale, no matter what you are making in your final sales.

Evaluate the options

Once you have taken the time to do your research on each product, you should be able to tell which one is the best for you. But you still need to consider which products are going to set you apart from some of the competition and even how you can add some value so the customer will choose you rather than choosing someone else for the same product.

Chapter 4: Choosing Your Products

The product that you pick will also help you to determine where you are going to sell them. If you are doing books or something like that, then Amazon can be a good option. But things like clothing and unique items may do better on Etsy. Having a good place to market your products can help you reach the right customers.

Check out the competition

This part may sound like it is counterintuitive, but it is a good idea to take some time to see what the competition in your niche is up to. You do not want to enter a market that has too much competition though, or you will waste a lot of time and effort. But you can always take a look at what your competition has been up to and use that to your advantage.

A good way to get started with this is to look at the pages of a few competitors in your niche. Pick out five or six that you would like to follow. Take some time to look through things on their page, whether it is through their own personal website or through another site like Amazon or eBay.

From here, the first thing that you will do is list out some things that you like about their page. What things do you think they do really well and you would like to use on your own page? What things are on the page that you would be attracted to and would make you purchase the product? Try to come up with at least a few things on each page to see what they are doing well with.

The next thing that you should do is look through the page and see what things you are not that fond of. What are things that kind of turn you off from the page or that you feel weren't done quite the right way? You should be able to find at least a few things on each competitor's page, no matter how well done the pages were, that turn you off and you can use this information to help better your page.

The point of this exercise is to determine what works and what does not work in your niche. You will be able to take the points that you liked and implement them into your website while making sure that you avoid the points that you were not that fond of. This helps you to create a page that is going to really highlight the products you want to sell while attracting the customers.

Picking out the product that you would like to use is a big deal when it comes to dropshipping. It is going to make a big difference on whether you are going to be able to sell a lot of products or even if you will make a decent amount of money from the products that you choose. Make sure to follow some of the tips that are in this chapter, and you are sure to find the right products that will take your new business to the top.

Chapter 5:

Which Sales Channels are the Best for My Business

Once you have decided on the niche that you would like to work with and what products you want to sell (as well as the supplier that you want to work with), it is time to determine the channels that you would like to use to sell these products. There are a lot of good places and channels that you can use to sell your products, but you should limit yourself to just a few of them, or you will stretch yourself too thin in the process.

The goal in this step is to find a good sales channel that is sure to put your products and services out in front of the right audience. And this is going to be determined by what kind of product you are selling. Some products are going to do better on eBay and others will do the best on Amazon or even your own personal website. You have to really understand the target audience that you are working with as well as the product to figure out the best place to sell these products. Here we are going to look at some of the different sales channels that you can choose and how they will work to put your product in front of the right customers.

eBay

The first channel that you should check out is eBay. This is one of the biggest online auction sites, and it can provide you with customers all over the world. It is also popular and many people who are looking for physical goods so you can easily get your information in front of a lot of people. Dropshipping on eBay is great because you get the advantage of having it be easy to start. You can set up an account and start selling instantly, so it does not take up a lot of time.

Another advantage of this is that it will allow you to access a big target audience. There are a lot of people who visit this site frequently for the products that they need. These buyers will be able to see the products that you are selling, and this can give it a lot of exposure. As long as you make sure that your products are listed at a good price, it is likely that you can make a good amount of sales.

Many beginners like this option because the platform will also take care of the marketing for them. eBay has a huge SEO background, so your products are sure to be found online without too much trouble. Since eBay is already well-known, you will not have to waste time or money trying to market your products if you list them on this site.

However, there are a few negatives to going with this option. You will notice that when you go to this channel, you will need to pay for listing your product. The cost is usually going to be ten percent of the selling price of all products. Since dropshipping usually does not have a huge margin of profit on the items that you sell, this large of a fee can make it impossible to make any money when you are using these sites.

Chapter 5: Which Sales Channels are the Best for My Business

Another issue that some dropshippers have is that they need to constantly monitor and relist the products that they are trying to sell, which can take up a lot of time and hassle. There is also a limitation on how much you can customize your page. You will be given a template by eBay, and it is hard to make your product stand out from all the others on this kind of site.

eBay can be a great platform to use to get started with your dropshipping business, but it is not always the best method to use. There are some benefits such as decreased marketing, but the fees that you have to pay and the lack of customization can make it hard to sell on these sites.

Amazon

Amazon is another sales channel that you can consider, and it is also a really popular marketplace. By listing your products on this site, you are going to get a lot of help in facilitating the sale while resolving issues that sometimes arise with it. It is also really easy to start out as a seller on Amazon since you just need to sign up for an account and you are ready to go.

Amazon also has a very large target audience that you can work with and the marketing, as well as the search engine optimization, are taken care of for you. Amazon also has its own warehouse that you can use if you would like to complement some of the items that you are selling.

There are a few drawbacks to using this as the sales channel though. There are going to be some listing fees involved in this, and you may find that this cuts into the profit that you can make. The fee that Amazon charges is going to vary based on the product type that you are trying to sell, but it will usually fall in the 15 to 20 percent range.

Another issue is that any sales data that you have done in the past is going to show up on your Amazon page. This can harm you in the beginning because you do not have a lot of backgrounds to show that you are a good seller to work with. It is also hard to form relationships with this kind of site and getting repeat customers is almost impossible.

Online store

Another option that you can go with is an online store. You will be able to set up your own website and then pick out some items that you would like to sell, especially if they are similar in nature, that you would like to sell on that website. It will cost a little bit of money to get the website up and running, and maybe a little bit to help keep it going if technical problems occur, but the costs are much lower than the other two options that we talked about, and this can be a great way to distinguish your products from the competition.

There is so much that you can do when you choose to pick out your own website. You can customize the site to go with the niche that you are offering to sell to. You can make sure that it is designed to your target audience rather than just having to fill out a template and hope that it all works out well. And since there are a lot of different online website designing companies, you can do it on your own or choose to have someone else help you to get it all started.

In addition to personalizing your dropshipping business and saving you some money, there is also the advantage of the

Chapter 5: Which Sales Channels are the Best for My Business

website being more mobile friendly compared to the other two options. With so many people turning to online to purchase their products, this is a really good thing. If you can make your website easy to use whether the person is on their computer or on their smartphone, you can really increase your own target audience.

However, there are a few downsides to having your own website and trying to sell products on there. There are literally hundreds of websites that are produced each day and getting yours to stand out from the crowd can seem impossible. It is not enough to just come up with a nice template and add a few products to the page; you also have to put in some work with SEO and other things to see results.

If you are not familiar with doing your own marketing and you do not know some of the secrets of the trade, then it is time to hire a professional. This does mean a little more in upfront costs, but it can help you so much when it comes to sales. Count it in as your advertising budget, and you will make money back in no time.

Other sites

The three sites that we talked about above are some of the most popular options to use when it comes to starting your own dropshipping business. But this does not mean that they are the only options that you can go with. Depending on the product that you are trying to sell, there are quite a few other sites that you can choose.

This is another place where you will have to do some research. There are a lot of options, such as Etsy if you are doing something that is handcrafted or homemade, but you are sure to find something that will work no matter what kind of product you are trying to sell.

Once you have determined what products you want to sell, go ahead and look online to figure out what auction sites, or other places, that you can use to sell them on. You may be surprised that there are a lot of options out there that are really popular, but that you had never heard about in the past, or at least had never thought about using. These can be great places to get your business started and will ensure that you are reaching the right target audience with your products.

Using social media

Using social media can be one of the best methods to selling your product. While it is not likely that you will just list and sell the products directly on these social media websites, it is possible to use social media to direct others back to your own personal website, or even to your eBay or Amazon page, to showcase what you are selling.

It is important to use social media in the right manner, or you are going to turn your customers off from you in no time. First, just pick out a few social media sites that you would like to work with. There are so many social media sites that are out there that it is easy to become overwhelmed and want to work with them all. But this is going to stretch you out too much and will waste too much of your time.

The best thing is to pick two or three social media sites where you think most of your audience is located. This is where you are going to spend most of your energy. You will want to learn

Chapter 5: Which Sales Channels are the Best for My Business

how to work those sites, what posts seem to get the most views and conversions, and what else that you need to do.

For example, Facebook is a good place for writing out more information on the product and having a longer description of the item, along with a decent picture, is one of the best ways to advertise on that platform. On the other hand, working on Pinterest or on Instagram is mostly picture related, so you will concentrate on higher quality images with just a little bit of text to go along with it.

Picking out the social media site can be a bit of a challenge, but take a look at your product. Do you think it would do well with a lot of pictures on it, would it do well with more text, or would something else set it apart from the crowd? Knowing your product as well as knowing the people who would purchase your product will help you to pick the right site.

While you are on social media, you need to make sure that you are active and that you interact with others on your page. You need to post on a regular basis, picking the time when your customers are most likely to be present and looking at the posts. This is going to take some research to figure out, but most social media sites will provide this to you so you can keep up on it.

When people ask questions or comment on your posts, you need to respond back in a timely manner. This does not mean that you have to answer right at that second and spend all day on your computer or your phone. Rather, it means that you need to be present and not make them wait for weeks to hear back. People like to feel that you notice them and that they matter to you as more than just a paycheck and interacting with them, even with something as simple as answering their questions and make a big difference.

Picking out a good social media site, posting on a regular basis with interesting material, and making sure that you interact with your customers are all great ways to ensure that you can put social media to work for you and actually make the sales that you would like.

Chapter 6:

Running Your Business

Getting started with your own drop shipping business can be a big undertaking, and there are going to be some challenges that come up along the way. However, if you have taken your time to learn about the industry, and you learn as much about it as you can, such as how to choose the right suppliers and the right niche to making sure everything is going to run as smoothly as possible, you are going to get the success that you would like.

The information that we have talked about in the rest of the guidebook is meant to provide you with some of the basics that you need to know to get started with your own dropshipping business. This business is a great way to get started, and so many people will use it as a part-time income, something to supplement their full-time income and to give them a little bit of savings to fall back on, in the beginning. But once they see how easy dropshipping can be, they will often switch it over to a full-time income and make more money than ever before.

This does not mean that dropshipping isn't going to take up some time and effort on your part. You need to be willing to put in some time to get the business up and running. While this business does send a lot of the work over to other people, such as the supplier who is going to ship your products, you still have to put in the work for marketing and selling those products to your audience. But once you get things started and you find the formula that works the best for your products, you could spend just a little bit of your day working in this business and making a good profit in the process.

Now that you have a good idea of how dropshipping works, it is time to look at some of the secrets that you should know to attain your success. These are some of the secrets that some of the best dropshippers will use to scale up their business and really see some results in no time. You can choose to mix and match some of these, based on your business model and the products that you plan to sell so that you get the best options for your needs.

Add in value

The first thing that you need to do when working on your dropshipping business is learning how to add value to the customer. No matter what kind of product you plan to sell, there are always going to be other competitors on the market who are going to try to sell the same product. How are you going to get your product to stand out from the crowd so that others will choose you instead of going with the competition?

Some people say that they will just lower their price and make that the most competitive thing about their site. This is not a good idea though. First, you are going to have some issues with making money off this option because your profit margins are already pretty low on most products. If you lower the price just to beat out the competition, it is likely that you

Chapter 6: Running Your Business

will not make any money in the process at all. Plus, many customers will see this lower price and wonder why you are offering it so low. They will assume that something is wrong with the product and will choose to go with another company who sells the same thing. Picking a price that is competitive in the market will make it easier to make some money in the process and won't scare away your customers at the same time.

With that being said, you need to find some other method to use to add value to your customer. Not only are customers looking for a product, but they are also often looking for insights, information, and solutions to their problems as well and if you can provide that to them, you can get so much more customers in the door.

So, with that in mind, you need to think of some ways that you and your product can solve a problem for your audience. Whether that includes adding a little booklet of recipes to your cooking products or some other information, making sure to add something a little special into the shipping, or something else, you have to make sure that you are providing your customer with an added value that they just cannot get anywhere else.

Add in some transparency

You need to make sure that there is a level of transparency in what you are doing with your customers. Customers do not like to feel fooled or like they are being taken advantage of when working with you, so showing as much transparency in your business as possible can be a big winner if you want to get ahead. This can sometimes be a little bit hard when you are working in the dropshipping business though because you do not gong to be the one that boxes up the products and sends them out to the customer.

But this is the perfect place to be transparent. You can let your customer know that someone else is going to be shipping the product to them. Some dropshippers shy away from doing this because they think it is going to show them in a bad light, but it is honestly going to make a huge difference in how much your customers trust you.

Prioritize the logistics

Another thing that you should focus on is logistics. The whole process of e-commerce fulfillment is going to involve choosing items in a fulfillment center and then directly shipping them over to the customers. This kind of business is also going to require you as the dropshipper to handle any of the issues that can come up after the order has been fulfilled. One of these issues can include returns on items.

With this in mind, it is important to ensure that you take logistics into consideration when you are planning on becoming a dropshipper. You and your suppliers need to have an agreement regarding the methods of fulfillment and the carriers to support, the average shipment time, the handling fees, and any issues with shipping. All of these are important to your customer, and if you think about them ahead of time, you can ensure that the supplier you are working with will provide great customer service for you.

If you take the time to talk about some of these logistics with your supplier before you get started, you are more likely to

Chapter 6: Running Your Business

succeed in your business. One other thing to consider about this logistics though is that you should remember that most consumers want to stick with shipping platforms that are simple and charges that are based on price.

Choose products that are unique

It is going to be hard for you to find some good customers and get their attention if you are not providing your customers with a product that is unique and something special. You can also work on creating a product catalog for your consumers if you would like, which is something that a lot of successful dropshippers will do to increase their reach and make it easier to make more money in the process. If you would like to see some success in this endeavor, you will need to take the time to understand that the data you generate from the vendors about the products you want to sell should only be your starting point.

There are some instances when the product descriptions that you are getting from your suppliers are actually written for the retailers, rather than for the customers, which can make it seem strange if you base your selling solely off these. What your next job is going to be will include changing these around, using the data that you are provided, and then enhance it and turn it into sales copy that will really entice your potential customers. This will help to make your products unique and can attract more customers in no time.

Also, you should remember that changing your product catalog is something that you should not do that often. Most of those who do well in dropshipping will stick with a manual process when it comes to picking out products, generating

45

content that is unique to describe these products, and then they will only make changes very rarely to help them look more professional and trustworthy. This does not mean that you cannot add some more products to your catalog over time, it is just not a good idea to do this all of the time.

Keep the price consistent

It is good customer service to ensure that you provide your audience with a product that comes in at a reasonable price. You still get the benefit of having control over the prices though. And there are going to be some instances when the final price is going to fluctuate, so you need to make sure that you are getting that control.

It is possible to keep that control while still making your audience happy. Let's take a look at eBay for example. This is often a bidding site where customers will choose how much they are willing to spend on something. But this does not mean that you do not have any control over the prices. Even on this site, you can set your minimum bid so that you are at least covering the costs of the product and making some profit in the process. This is a great way to make sure that the price is agreeable to both you and the customer.

Make sure that the product is available

If you want to make your customers happy with working with your business, then you need to make sure that your product is always available to them. If they are always waiting for a product or they purchase it, wait a few days, and then find out that the product is no longer in stock, they are not going to be

Chapter 6: Running Your Business

happy. And since you are the person they are working with, you will receive the bad reviews, not the manufacturer

So, it is always in your best interest to make sure that the products are in stock as much as possible. There may be sometimes, such as with seasonal items, that you cannot do it well, but you should try to keep up with the stock levels that your wholesaler is sending to you. This will give you some time to see that an item is almost out of stock and you can choose to delist it until it comes back to avoid this issue.

Picking out a good wholesaler to work with can make a difference as well. If the wholesaler has some bad reviews that state how they are not doing a good job keeping up with their orders or they cancel orders on a frequent basis, it is not a good idea to go with this company. Always look for wholesalers that keep up with their inventory and will provide your customers with the best experience possible.

Build up some good relationships

You need to make sure that you are developing some good relationships with both sides of this business. You need these good relationships with your customers as well as with your suppliers. Doing this is going to make it easier to earn a higher profit on your products because both parties will trust you and will work with you to get the job done.

When you get a great relationship going with your wholesaler, you get the benefit of knowing you are working with a company who is going to take care of you. They will fulfill your orders, will make sure that the product is high-quality and is going to last for a very long time, and they can help make your job with customer service a little bit easier.

But you also need to concentrate on forming a good relationship with your customers. Remember that there are a lot of competitors out there who also want to be able to get the same sales that you are going for. Building up a good relationship with these customers will make it easier or you to get them to come to your store in the first place, and it can result in repeat customers and good referrals, which can be amazing for growing your business.

So, how do you go about making sure that you are providing this good relationship with your customers? We have taken some time to talk about a few ideas already in this guidebook, you just need to be able to implement them into your business, and you are ready to get started. Make sure that you fulfill the orders quickly, you respond back to any questions or concerns that the customer may have, and you make sure that you are providing them with some value in the process. If you can do this and do it well, you are going to see results in no time.

There are many people who want to get into the dropshipping business, but not all of them are going to be a success. Sure, dropshipping can be a great passive income if you work at it, but you also have to make sure that you are putting in the time and effort to really showcase those products and to provide the customer service that your customers are looking for. If you can put all of this together, you are going to see the great results that you are looking for.

Conclusion

Thank you for making it through to the end of this book, let's hope it was informative and able to provide you with all of the tools you need to achieve your goals whatever they may be.

The next step is to get started with running your own dropshipping business. This is not a business that everyone is going to be able to do well in. Sure, anyone can pick out a good supplier and get started, but it does take a lot of hard work and some dedication to see results. The good news is that if you can keep up with the work and pick out the right products, you are going to see results and you will not have to do a ton of work once it is up and running.

This guidebook took some time to discuss dropshipping and some of the basics that you need to know to get started. We took a look at what dropshipping is all about and some of the benefits that come with it, how to pick out a good supplier to work with, how to choose the right products that will sell and make you some profit in the process, and even how to pick the right sales channel. When you are done with this guidebook, you are sure to have all the answers that you need to start your own dropshipping company and see some great results.

When you are ready to earn some money on the side, or you want to turn this into a full-time business, make sure to check out this guidebook and learn how to get started with dropshipping today.

Finally, if you found this book useful in any way, a review on Amazon is always appreciated.

www.ingramcontent.com/pod-product-compliance
Lightning Source LLC
Chambersburg PA
CBHW040241220526
45473CB00001B/326